# A Note to Parents

DK READERS is a compelling program for beginning readers, designed in conjunction with leading literacy experts, including Dr. Linda Gambrell, Professor of Education at Clemson University. Dr. Gambrell has served as President of the National Reading Conference and the College Reading Association, and has recently been elected to serve as President of the International Reading Association.

Beautiful illustrations and superb full-color photographs combine with engaging, easy-to-read text to offer a fresh approach to each subject in the series. Each DK READER is guaranteed to capture a child's interest while developing his or her reading skills, general knowledge, and love of reading.

The five levels of DK READERS are aimed at different reading abilities, enabling you to choose the books that are exactly right for your child:

**Pre-level 1:** Learning to read
**Level 1:** Beginning to read
**Level 2:** Beginning to read alone
**Level 3:** Reading alone
**Level 4:** Proficient readers

The "normal" age at which a child begins to read can be anywhere from three to eight years old, so these levels are only a general guideline.

No matter which level you select, you can be sure that you are helping your child learn to read, then read to learn!

LONDON, NEW YORK, MUNICH,
MELBOURNE, AND DELHI

**Senior Editor** Catherine Saunders
**Designer** Sandra Perry
**Brand Manager** Lisa Lanzarini
**Publishing Manager** Simon Beecroft
**Category Publisher** Siobhan Williamson
**DTP Designer** Santosh Kumar Ganapathula
**Production** Nick Seston
**Reading Consultant**
Linda Gambrell

**Lucasfilm Ltd.**
**Executive Editor** Jonathan Rinzler
**Art Director** Troy Alders
**Continuity Editor** Leland Chee
**Director of Publishing** Carol Roeder

First published in the United States in 2007 by
DK Publishing
375 Hudson Street
New York, New York 10014

07 08 09 10 11 10 9 8 7 6 5 4 3 2 1
SD299 – 05/07

DK Books are available at special discounts when
purchased in bulk for sales promotions, premiums,
fund-raising, or educational use.
For details, contact: DK Publishing Special Markets,
375 Hudson Street, New York, New York 10014
SpecialSales@dk.com

A catalog record for this book is available
from the Library of Congress.

ISBN: 978-0-7566-3114-7 (paperback)
ISBN: 978-0-7566-3115-4 (hardback)

Color reproduction by GRB Editrice S.r.l., London
Printed and bound by L-Rex, China.

starwars.com/fan

Discover more at
www.dk.com

# Contents

# DK READERS

LUCAS BOOKS

# STAR WARS™

# BEWARE THE
# DARK SIDE

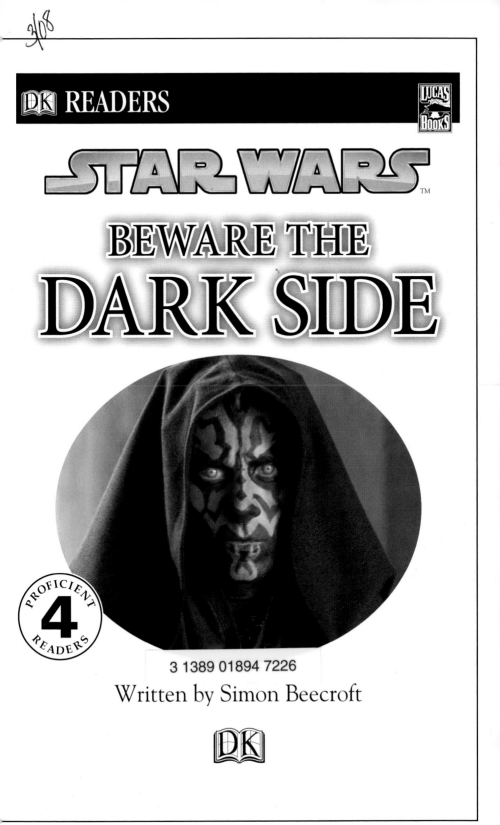

PROFICIENT **4** READERS

3 1389 01894 7226

Written by Simon Beecroft

DK

## The Force
The Force is an invisible energy created by all living things. A few people with special powers can control the Force. The Force is mostly a good energy, but it also has a dark side that can be used for evil.

# Faces of Evil

A long time ago, the galaxy was ruled by an evil man named Darth Sidious (pronounced SID-EE-US). He was also known as Emperor Palpatine (pronounced PAL-PA-TEEN). He used fear, corruption, and the dark side of the Force to rule his evil Empire.

*Emperor Palpatine*

Darth Sidious's special abilities made him very powerful. He used the dark side of the Force to control people's minds and events. He also used the dark side to throw heavy objects with his mind, and to fire a deadly lightning from his fingers.

In these pages, you will meet many villains who used the dark side of the Force to do terrible things. You will also meet evildoers who did not use the Force, but who were still on the side of darkness. Finally, you will meet the brave few who dared to stand up to the dark side.

The Jedi order
Jedi Master Obi-Wan Kenobi said that the Force "surrounds us, penetrates us, and binds the galaxy together". The Jedi are a group of individuals who devote their lives to using the Force for good. The Jedi protect people and keep peace in the galaxy.

**Sith lightsabers**
Each Jedi builds his or her own weapon called a lightsaber. They are made from glowing energy crystals. Sith lightsaber blades are usually red.

# Sith Lord

Darth Sidious was a Sith Lord. The Sith had been around for many centuries. The first Sith was a Jedi who turned to the dark side. Others followed him. Together they tried to destroy the Jedi. The Sith even tried to kill each other because they were so full of evil and hatred. The Jedi thought they had destroyed the Sith. But, one Sith survived. He took an apprentice and went into hiding. Since then, the Sith have plotted revenge on the Jedi.

The Sith were the Jedi's most feared enemies. The Sith used the dark side of the Force to gain terrible powers. Like the Jedi, they fought with a lightsaber, which is a sword whose blade is made of pure energy. The Sith and the Jedi were the only people in the galaxy who used lightsabers. The lightsaber was the ancient weapon of the Jedi, but since the Sith were once Jedi, they used them too.

**Lightsabers**
The handle contains special crystals that make the energy blade appear when needed. Jedi lightsaber blades are either blue, green, or purple.

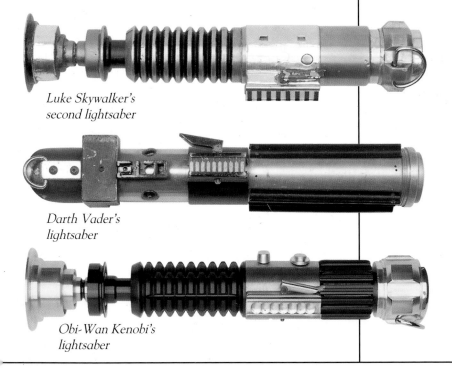

*Luke Skywalker's second lightsaber*

*Darth Vader's lightsaber*

*Obi-Wan Kenobi's lightsaber*

# Sith Powers

The Sith believed that the dark side of the Force was more powerful than the light. Turning to the dark side seemed to bring results quickly, while the Jedi had to patiently study the light side of the Force for many years. The Sith also rejected the Jedi's teachings that emotions must be controlled. They used anger and hatred to become stronger, but the Sith had no loyalty and were often destroyed by the dark side.

**Evil temptation**
The Jedi understood that the dark side was a powerful temptation for all Jedi. Most managed to resist it, but a few gave in to its evil powers.

In battle, the Sith tried
to crush their opponents
with heavy objects, which
they threw using their dark
side energies.

The dark side of the Force gave
the Sith powers that the Jedi did not
have. One of them was deadly Force
lightning. They could fire it from
their fingers at an opponent.
However, this power was very
dangerous and could also harm
the user.

**Force lightning**
When Sidious
attacked a Jedi
called Mace
Windu with
Force lightning,
Mace threw it
back at Sidious.
The lightning
hit Sidious's
face and scarred
it forever.

When the galaxy was united in peace, a Galactic Republic was formed. It was a democracy, which meant that every person in nearly all the worlds had a voice.

# The Phantom Menace

Before Darth Sidious became Emperor of the galaxy, he was a popular politician called Senator Palpatine. At this time, the galaxy was at peace and laws were made in the Senate. All the different planets had a voice in the Senate and large armies were outlawed.

Palpatine secretly wanted to take over the galaxy. He planned to destroy the Senate and build a massive army so that he could force every planet to do what he wanted.

No one suspected that Palpatine was really a Sith Lord. After he secretly started a war in the galaxy, Palpatine convinced the Senate to make him their leader, the Supreme Chancellor. Then he gave himself the power to make all the decisions. Finally, he crowned himself Emperor. Now the dark side ruled the galaxy.

**The Senate**
The Senate was a gigantic circular building on the galaxy's capital planet, Coruscant.

**Secret Sith**
Palpatine hid his true Sith identity from the Senate.

# Jedi Defenders

When the Sith revealed themselves after two thousand years in hiding, only the Jedi had the powers to face them. The Jedi vow to use their Force powers only to do good. The good side of the Force is known as the light side.

Learning to use the light side of the Force takes many years. Those who become Jedi begin training as young children. They must leave their families behind and live in the Jedi Temple on a big planet.

**Yoda**
Yoda was the wisest Jedi of all. He was hundreds of years old when the Sith reappeared.

The Jedi learn to control their emotions so that they can remain calm and practical in all situations. The Jedi seek to keep the Force in balance in the galaxy, which means that they must stop those who seek to use the dark side.

The Jedi can actually listen to the Force telling them that there is trouble happening somewhere. This is known as a disturbance in the Force. It means there's a problem some place in the galaxy— and the Jedi must find it and do whatever they can to stop it.

**Obi-Wan**
Obi-Wan Kenobi was a powerful Jedi. While the Sith ruled the galaxy, Obi-Wan went into hiding. Yoda also went into hiding.

**Jedi Council**
The wisest, most experienced Jedi sat on the Jedi High Council. Before the Sith attacked, Yoda felt great disturbances in the Force, but even he was not able to see where the threat came from.

# Darth Vader

Darth Vader ruled the galaxy alongside Darth Sidious. Vader was also a Sith Lord. His knowledge of the dark side of the Force made him a powerful and dangerous figure. Vader would kill anyone who got in his way or disobeyed him, even his own generals. He used his Force powers to strangle people without even touching them.

**Masked man**
Vader's armor and breathing equipment were created in a secret medical facility.

**Vader uncovered**
Vader removed his helmet only in a special isolation chamber. Mechanical arms lifted the helmet from his scarred head.

Darth Vader always
wore a black suit of
armor and a black
mask because his body
had been almost
destroyed in a great
battle. His armor and mask
contained breathing equipment and
life-support systems to keep him
alive. The wheezing sound of
Vader's artificial breathing was
enough to strike terror into the mind
of anyone he approached.

**Space fighter**
Vader flew his
own fighter ship
into combat.
He was a very
daring pilot.

**Lightsaber duel**
Vader was a
merciless
opponent in
battle, and did
not hesitate to
cut down his
former Master,
Obi-Wan
Kenobi.

# Anakin Skywalker

Before he became a Sith Lord, Darth Vader was a Jedi called Anakin Skywalker. Anakin was one of the most talented Jedi ever. His Force powers were incredibly strong, but Anakin was impatient.

He wanted to become more powerful than any other Jedi.

Palpatine befriended Anakin and began to plant ideas in his mind.

He convinced Anakin to join him on the dark side and train to be a Sith. Palpatine told Anakin that the dark side of the Force was more powerful than the light side. He even told Anakin that he would be able to stop his wife from dying. Anakin wanted this more than anything, so he rejected his Jedi training and joined Palpatine.

When Anakin joined the dark side, he killed many Jedi. He even fought his best friend, Obi-Wan Kenobi. On the edge of a lava river, Anakin and Obi-Wan fought fiercely until Obi-Wan managed to strike down his former friend. Anakin fell near the red-hot lava and burst into flames. Palpatine rescued him, and re-built his badly burned body with robotic parts and a suit of armor—and Darth Vader was born!

**Padmé Amidala**
Anakin secretly married the Senator for Naboo, Padmé Amidala, even though the Jedi are forbidden to marry.

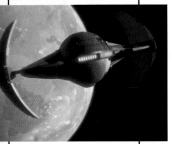

# Maul

Each Sith Master chose a
single apprentice, whom he
trained in the dark side. Sidious
first chose a savage alien from the
planet Iridonia. Given the Sith name
Darth Maul, he served his master
obediently, although he was only
waiting for the day when he would
take Sidious's place. Maul
had horns on his head
and yellow eyes. His
face was tattooed
with dark side
symbols. Maul's
weapon was a
double-bladed
lightsaber.

When two Jedi named Qui-Gon
Jinn (pronounced KWY-GONN-
JIN) and Obi-Wan Kenobi
(pronounced OH-BEE-ONE KEN-
OH-BEE) started to upset Sidious's
plans, he sent Maul to kill them.
The fight took place on the edge
of a giant power generator
on Palpatine's home planet,
Naboo. The Jedi were not
prepared for such a ferocious
attack. Qui-Gon was killed,
but Obi-Wan defeated the
deadly Sith apprentice.

**Sith Master**
Sidious kept in
contact with his
apprentice using
a hologram
transmitter.

# Count Dooku

Sidious needed a new apprentice after Obi-Wan killed Darth Maul on Naboo. His search led him to Count Dooku, who was once a Jedi Master. Although he joined the Jedi order at a young age, Dooku was interested in the dark side and wanted power to change things quickly. When Dooku joined Sidious, he took the new Sith name—
Darth Tyranus.

**Weapon**
Tyranus's weapon was a lightsaber with a curved handle. His special moves could surprise even the most experienced Jedi.

*Count Dooku*

For many years, Dooku had been encouraging planets and business organizations to leave the Senate and build droid armies. He told them that this would make the galaxy a better place. In reality he was doing only what Sidious told him to do. He did not know what Sidious's true plans were.

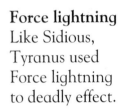

**Force lightning**
Like Sidious, Tyranus used Force lightning to deadly effect.

Sidious eventually betrayed Dooku and allowed him to be killed by Anakin Skywalker. Sidious knew that the powerful and gifted Anakin would be a more useful Sith apprentice than Dooku.

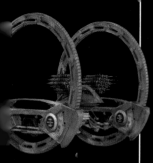

# Droid Army

Count Dooku had persuaded many planets and organizations to buy powerful droid armies. The footsoldiers were blaster-wielding battle droids while heavily armored super battle droids provided backup. Hailfire droids rolled across the battlefields, each equipped with deadly cannon or missile launchers. Deadly machines called droideka were used on special missions.

**Hailfire droids**
Hailfire droids are shaped like massive wheels. They can race across flat ground or shallow lakes, flattening anything in their path.

**Tri-fighter**
Tri-fighters seek
out and hunt
down enemy
ships in space,
training their
deadly nose
cannons on
their prey.

Heavily armed droid ships were
also used for space battles. They
included vulture droids, which could
also walk along the ground, and tri-
fighters. Swarms of tiny buzz droids
attached themselves to
enemy ships. Although
they were very small,
their cutting and sawing
arms could inflict
serious damage.

**Spider droids**
Spider droids go
into battle
equipped with
heat-seeking
missiles.

# General Grievous

With the outbreak of war in the galaxy, many brutal fiends joined the Sith Lords. One such recruit was General Grievous, a warlord whose battle-scarred body had been rebuilt with cyborg parts. The only parts of his original body left were his reptile-like eyes and his inner organs, which were protected by armor. Although he was more machine than man, Grievous would kill anyone who called him a droid.

**Bodyguards**
Grievous was accompanied by droid bodyguards, who were equipped with deadly energy staffs.

Grievous became Supreme Commander of the droid armies. Dooku taught Grievous to use a lightsaber, although Grievous could not use the Force like the Sith and Jedi.

Grievous had a long-standing grudge against the Jedi, and took the lightsabers of any Jedi he killed. In battle, Grievous could split his two arms into four, each of which could wield a lightsaber. He also used a deadly blaster and a powerful energy staff, which delivered fatal electric shocks to his opponents.

**Final battle**
Grievous was no match for the combined power of the Jedi Obi-Wan Kenobi and Anakin Skywalker.

# Clone Soldiers

Although Sidious had started a war in the galaxy, he didn't want either side to win it. He wanted the war to go on just long enough for him to bring the Sith to power. He made sure that the Republic had an army of its own, so that each side was evenly matched. The Republic army consisted of well-trained clone soldiers and a variety of battle tanks, plus cannons, gunships, and space assault ships.

**Special training**
Each clone trooper was an identical copy of a single "supreme soldier" named Jango Fett. Each clone was grown in a factory and trained for combat from birth.

**Battle vehicles**
In battle, clone troopers operated several kinds of tank and flew armed gunships.

For many battles, the clone soldiers fought on the side of the Republic. The Jedi generals did not know that the clone soldiers were programmed to be loyal to Sidious. When Sidious gave a special signal, the clone soldiers turned on their Republic masters, showing no mercy.

**Weapons**
Clone troopers carried powerful blasters and rifles.

# Stormtroopers

When the war was over, Darth Sidious ruled the galaxy as Emperor Palpatine, and the clone soldiers became his personal army.
He renamed them stormtroopers and forced many millions of human males to join their ranks. Military Academies were formed in which new recruits were trained to be foot soldiers or more specialized troops, such as pilots or scouts. The stormtroopers were trained to be totally loyal to the Empire.

**Armor**
Stormtrooper armor protected the soldier inside from weapon and bomb blasts.

*Stormtrooper*

The stormtroopers could not be bribed or persuaded into betraying the Emperor. People everywhere learned to fear the sinister white-armored troops.

**Snowtroopers**
Some stormtroopers wore specialized armor to protect them from the cold on freezing planets. They were called snowtroopers.

**Vader's son**
Luke was raised on Anakin's home planet, Tatooine, by his uncle and aunt.

**Vader's daughter**
Leia was raised on the planet Alderaan. She became a Princess—and a secret member of the Rebel Alliance.

# Empire and Rebels

When Darth Sidious came to power, a dark age began in the galaxy—the Empire. As Emperor Palpatine, Sidious used his massive armies to terrify the galaxy and to stop anyone from rising against him.

Nevertheless, a secret opposition was formed, called the Rebel Alliance. The most famous Rebels were the children of Darth Vader, Luke and Leia.

When Anakin Skywalker turned to the dark side, he did not know that his wife, Padmé Amidala, was pregnant with twins. Tragically, Padmé died while giving birth. The twins were hidden away in separate places, so that Anakin would not find out about them.

**Rebel Alliance**
Leia and the Rebel Alliance plan an attack on the Empire from their secret base on the planet Yavin 4.

**Han Solo**
The Rebels welcomed any support they could get, even from former smugglers like Han Solo and Chewbacca.

# Jango Fett

The first clone troopers were cloned from a single "supreme warrior." He was a man named Jango Fett. Jango made his living as a bounty hunter. This means that he was paid to hunt criminals and outlaws. Darth Tyranus knew of his unbeatable combat skills and recruited him for the secret clone-army project.

*Jango Fett*

Jango also carried out certain special missions for the Sith Lords. For example, he would assassinate any public figures that stood between the Sith Lords and their ultimate goal of ruling the galaxy. One such person was the good Senator Padmé Amidala. Thankfully, Padmé survived the attempts on her life, and the Jedi pursued Jango. Eventually, Jango was killed in a large battle between the Republic army and the droid army.

**Jetpack**
Jango uses his jetpack to attack Jedi Obi-Wan from above.

**Flame thrower**
Jango fires his deadly wrist-mounted flame thrower.

# Zam Wesell

Jango Fett had many contacts in the criminal underworld. One such contact was the hired assassin Zam Wesell. Zam was an alien whose species could shape-shift, which meant that she could change her body shape to imitate other species. This was useful when she needed to blend in with another planet's species without being noticed.

**Airspeeder**
When Zam needed to make a fast getaway, she jumped into her fast, green airspeeder.

Jango hired Zam to carry out the daring murder of the politician Senator Padmé Amidala. First Zam tried to blow up the Senator's spaceship. Then, she released deadly insects called kouhuns into Padmé's bedroom while she slept, but her Jedi bodyguards were able to stop the attack in time. Zam was chased by the Jedi Obi-Wan Kenobi and Anakin Skywalker. They managed to capture her, but before she could give anything away, she was shot by a mysterious figure in the shadows—Jango Fett.

**Jedi protector**
Obi-Wan was trying to protect Senator Amidala.

**True face**
When shape-shifters die, they return to their own body shape.

# Boba Fett

When Jango Fett was killed in battle, he left a young son named Boba. Young Boba had spent his whole life learning from his father, so when he grew up, he too became a bounty hunter. Boba inherited his father's armor and weapons, and became the best bounty hunter in the galaxy. Boba often worked for Darth Vader, tracking down enemies of the Empire.

When Darth Vader learned that he had a son, he wanted to track him down and see if he could turn him to the dark side. He would have liked to rule the galaxy alongside his son.

**Like father, like son**
Boba Fett is an exact, unaltered clone of his father, Jango.

**Secret weapons**
Boba's armor conceals a deadly flame thrower and powerful rocket dart launchers.

Vader employed Boba Fett to find and capture Luke, but Luke was firmly on the side of good. He had begun to train as a Jedi and refused to turn to the dark side.

Boba was eventually defeated during a battle with Luke Skywalker and his allies. Boba Fett's jetpack was damaged, causing it to malfunction. It sent the bounty hunter soaring into the air, out of control. Fett finally tumbled to his death into the ravenous jaws of a giant desert creature called the Sarlacc.

**Armed spaceship**
Boba traveled in his father's ship, "Slave I". The ship was full of weapons.

**Possible escape**
Some people believe that Boba managed to escape from the stomach of the Sarlacc.

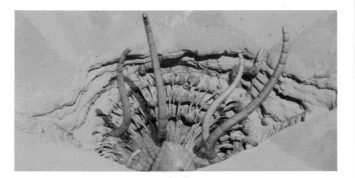

# Jabba the Hutt

Another of Boba Fett's employers was a crime lord named Jabba the Hutt. This repellent slug-like creature was the leader of a large crime empire responsible for all kinds of shady deals, including murder, theft, and fraud. Jabba lived in a palace on the desert planet Tatooine. He shared his palace with assorted gangsters, assassins, smugglers, corrupt officials, low-life entertainers, and servants

Jabba paid Boba Fett
to bring him a smuggler
who owed him money.
That smuggler was
Han Solo, who had
become friends with
Luke and Leia
Skywalker. When Han was captured
and brought to Jabba, Leia set out
with Chewbacca to rescue Han.
When she was also captured, it was
up to Luke to rescue all his friends.
During Luke's rescue mission, Leia
was able to wrap a chain around
Jabba's neck and defeat him.

**Bib Fortuna**
Bib Fortuna ran
Jabba's palace
for him. He had
a large head
tail, sharp teeth,
and scary red
eyes.

**Pet monster**
Jabba kept
a ferocious
rancor monster
in a cellar pit.
Sometimes he
fed it human
captives for fun.

# Rogues and Villains

Even before the Empire took control, parts of the galaxy were wild and lawless. On remote planets like Tatooine, highly dangerous Podraces were organized, although they were officially banned. Slavery was also common. When the Jedi Qui-Gon visited Tatooine, he met a slave dealer named Watto. Watto owned Anakin Skywalker and his mother, Shmi. Anakin and Shmi both worked for Watto in his junk shop.

**Informer**
Garindan was a low-life informer who lived on Tatooine.

**Watto**
Watto made Anakin and Shmi work very hard.

Under the Empire, crime was often rewarded. The Empire relied on spies to report suspicious behavior. Often, it forced officials to do its shady business.

When Darth Vader wanted to capture Luke Skywalker, he threatened to shut down an entire city if its leader, Lando Calrissian, did not lure Luke into a trap. When Vader broke his promise, Lando helped Luke and joined the Rebels.

**Calrissian**
Lando Calrissian had great charm.

**Greedo**
Greedo was a small-time hitman hired to kill Han Solo.

# Imperial Migh

The Empire kept control of the galaxy with its gigantic army of stormtroopers and a fleet of warships that patrolled all the major space routes. The biggest warship was Darth Vader's personal ship, the "Executor." The "Executor" led a fleet of Star Destroyers.

**Heavy weapons**
Star Destroyers were armed with many powerful weapons.

Each Star Destroyer had
enough firepower to destroy entire
planets. Swarming around these
big ships were countless smaller
TIE-fighters, each piloted by a
fighter pilot.

When the Empire discovered a
Rebel secret base on the ice planet
Hoth, it sent in massive walking
tanks called AT-ATs. Pilots
controlled the tanks from a cockpit
in the head. Until the battle of
Hoth, AT-ATs were thought to be
unbeatable in battle, but the
Rebels toppled them
by wrapping cables
around their legs.

**Scout walkers**
Smaller AT-ST,
or scout
walkers,
patrolled
many planets.

**Sinister spy**
A probe droid
spotted the
Rebel base on
Hoth and
informed the
Empire.

43

**Torture**
Onboard the
Death Star,
Darth Vader
threatened to
use a torture
droid on
Princess Leia
to make her
reveal the
whereabouts of
the Rebel bases.

# Death Star

The Death Star was the Emperor's
most terrifying superweapon. It was
the size of small moon, but it was
actually one of the largest starships
ever built. Its gigantic superlaser
weapon could destroy entire planets.
To demonstrate its enormous power,
the Empire used it to
destroy the planet of
Alderaan. This was
the planet on which
Darth Vader's
daughter, Leia, had
lived most of her life.

**Fatal flaw**
The unguarded exhaust port was located at the end of a long channel on the surface of the Death Star.

Yet even the Death Star had a flaw. If a skilled pilot could fire torpedoes into a small exhaust shaft on the Death Star's surface, a chain reaction of explosions would blow up the entire starship. The Rebel Alliance sent their best pilots to reach the target. Luke Skywalker trusted in the Force and fired. A direct hit! Luke had managed to destroy the Empire's most terrible weapon.

**Mastermind**
One of the Emperor's leaders, Grand Moff Tarkin, was the mastermind behind the Death Star.

# Rebel Victory

The brave Rebels refused to give up the fight against Emperor Palpatine and his Empire of evil. Although the Emperor commanded the biggest army in the galaxy, he was not invincible. The Rebels teamed up with a band of forest-dwelling creatures called Ewoks on the planet Endor. Together they overpowered the Emperor's stormtroopers and helped the Rebels' spaceships to launch a full-scale attack on the second Death Star.

**Second Death Star**
After the Rebels destroyed the first Death Star, Emperor Palpatine ordered that a replacement be built.

**Look out!**
The Ewoks only used weapons made of wood, yet they managed to defeat the well-trained and well-armed stormtroopers.

Meanwhile onboard the Death Star, Luke battled for his life against the Emperor and Darth Vader. When Luke refused to turn to the dark side, the Emperor forced the father and son to fight. In the end, Luke could not kill Vader and when the Emperor tried to kill Luke, Vader turned against his Sith Master and threw him to his doom down a deep shaft.

Luke had proven that even those who have turned to the dark side still have good inside them that can be reached—if you only know how.

**Vader unmasked**
Luke lifted Vader's mask to gaze at the face of the father he had never known.

# Glossary

**Apprentice**
A person who is learning a skill.

**Blaster**
A gun that fires a deadly beam of light.

**Bounty hunter**
A person who hunts criminals and other wanted people, in return for money.

**Clone**
An exact copy of another person.

**Dark side**
The part of the Force associated with fear and hatred.

**Droid**
A kind of robot.

**Emperor**
The leader of an Empire is called an Emperor. Palpatine is the Emperor who rules the Galactic Empire.

**Empire**
A group of nations ruled by one leader.

**The Force**
An energy field created by all living things.

**Force lightning**
One of the Sith's powers which involved firing deadly electricity from their fingers.

**Galactic**
Something from or to do with a galaxy.

**Galaxy**
A group of millions of stars and planets.

**Jedi Council**
The governing body of the Jedi order. The wisest Jedi, such as Yoda, sit on the Council.

**Jedi Knight**
A *Star Wars* warrior with special powers who defends the good of the galaxy. Anakin Skywalker, Luke Skywalker, and Ob-Wan Kenobi are all Jedi Knights.

**Jedi Master**
The most experienced Jedi of all.

**Jedi order**
The name of a group that defends peace and justice in the galaxy.

**Jedi Temple**
The Jedi headquarters where the Jedi Council meets and Jedi live, train, and work.

**Lightsaber**
A Jedi's or Sith's weapon, made of glowing energy.

**Light side**
The part of the Force associated with goodness, compassion, and healing

**Rebel**
Someone who opposes whoever is in power.

**Republic**
A nation or group of nations in which the people vote for their leaders.

**Senate**
The governing body of the Republic.

**Senator**
A member of the Senate. He or she will have been chosen (elected) by the people of his or her country.

**Sith**
Enemies of the Jedi who use the dark side of the Force.

**Stormtroopers**
Soldiers, many of them clones, who are loyal to Emperor Palpatine. They wear white armor.